Brady's Guide to Navigating the Internet

Second Edition

Matthew R. Streger, BA, NREMT-P

Paramedic
Greenville County EMS
Greenville, South Carolina

Brady/Prentice Hall
Upper Saddle River, New Jersey 07458

Publisher: *Susan Katz*
Acquisitions editor: *Judy Streger*
Marketing manager: *Tiffany Price*
Marketing coordinator: *Cindy Frederick*
Director of production and manufacturing: *Bruce Johnson*
Managing production editor: *Patrick Walsh*
Editorial/production supervision, interior design,
    and page layout: *Julie Boddorf*
Senior production manager: *Ilene Sanford*
Creative director: *Marianne Frasco*
Cover design: *Miguel Ortiz*

© 1999, 1997 by Prentice-Hall, Inc.
Simon & Schuster / A Viacom Company
Upper Saddle River, New Jersey 07458

Printed in the United States of America
10 9 8 7 6 5 4 3

ISBN 0-8359-5324-6

The first edition of this volume was written by Andrew T. Stull and adapted for Brady by
Michael R. Gunderson.

Windows, Windows 95, Internet Explorer, and NetMeeting are registered trademarks of
the Microsoft Corporation. Macintosh is a registered trademark of Apple Computer.
America Online (AOL) is a registered trademark of America Online. CompuServe is a
registered trademark of CompuServe Interactive Services. Prodigy is a registered trademark of Prodigy Services Corporation. AT&T is a registered trademark of AT&T
Corporation. MCI is a registered trademark of MCI Telecommunications. UUNet is a registered trademark of UUNet Technologies. Netcom On-Line Communication Services is a
registered trademark of ICG Communications. Netscape Navigator is a registered trademark of Netscape Communications. Yahoo! is a registered trademark of Yahoo!
Corporation. Excite is a registered trademark of Excite Corporation. Lycos is a registered
trademark of the Lycos Corporation. Infoseek is a registered trademark of Infoseek
Corporation. Juno is a registered trademark of Juno Online Services. Hotmail is a regis-
tered trademark of Hotmail Corporation. CNN is a registered trademark of Cable News
Network. ICQ is a registered trademark of Mirablis. Eudora is a registered trademark of
Qualcomm Corporation. Windows95.com is a registered trademark of Jenesys, LLC.
Mobile Healthcare Forum is a registered trademark of the Institute for Prehospital
Medicine. Emergency.net is a registered trademark of Emergency Response and Research
Institute. MERGINet is a registered trademark of MERGINet Medical Resources. EMBBS
is a registered trademark of Triple Star Systems. HealthAtoZ.com is a registered trade-
mark of Medical Network. NAEMT is a registered trademark of the National Association
of Emergency Medical Technicians. JEMS is a registered trademark of Mosby. EMS
Magazine is a registered trademark of Summer Communications.

The author and publisher of this manual have used their best efforts in preparing this
book. The author and publisher make no warranty of any kind, expressed or implied,
with regard to these programs or the documentation contained in this book. The author
and publisher shall not be liable in any event for incidental or consequential damages in
connection with, or arising out of, the furnishing, performance, or use of the programs
described in this book.

Contents

Chapter 1

Introduction

Internet History

The Internet can be a very intimidating place. It is a classic case of the "haves" and the "have-nots." Those who have Internet access speak a special language and often know about things before everyone else. Those who do not have Internet access can feel left out in the cold, without information or contacts that may be essential for their business. This is not to say that the Internet is an easy place to navigate—it can be confusing, frustrating, and complicated.

The Internet as we know it now was born in 1969 as a group of computers from different colleges and universities around the country. You may have noticed that many people who have Internet access are from schools. This is because that's where it all started. The only problem was getting all these different computers to speak the same language. The U.S. government sponsored the solution, which is a universal language for all computers on the Internet to use. This language is called *transmission control protocol / Internet protocol* (TCP/IP).

The Internet is just a way of connecting many different computers throughout the world. Nobody controls the Internet though a central group controls *domain names*. These are the individual names of each computer that is connected to the Internet. Names are automatically converted into *DNS* entries, which are four groups of numbers separated by periods. Domain names as we use them are issued by a central agency. They usually have the computer name based on the company, school, or organization that owns it, followed by the type of agency. You may see types such as *edu* for schools and universities, *com* for commercial establishments, *org* for non-profit organizations, and *gov* for government agencies.

There are two important concepts to understand regarding the Internet: *client–server networks* and *packet data transfer*. The client–server network exists where a computer (client) requests a file or piece of information from a central computer (server). In this way, many computers can share up-to-date information without having to update files on each individual client computer. The Internet is just an enormous client–server network, where your home computer requests information from servers around the world.

Packet data transfer is the method by which information is transmitted from computer to computer on the Internet. A message, like an e-mail, is sent from computer A to computer B. It is not transmitted directly from computer A to computer B. Rather, it is broken down into packets, small pieces of the original message, and bounced through many servers along the way. Different packets may take different routes to the destination. In this way, a roadblock at one server along the way will not prevent the message from being sent. It will just take another route and be reassembled at the end.

There are several different functions of the Internet. The most simple is electronic mail, or *e-mail*. E-mail is just a simple method of sending a message from one person to another. *Newsgroups* are public forums for posting messages for everyone to read and reply to on a specific subject. Newsgroups are also known as Usenet. These are all simple, text-based functions. Most early Internet work was done in a text language called *UNIX,* and some Internet connections are still in UNIX. However, the explosion of growth on the Internet is related to the development of *Hypertext Markup Language* (HTML) in 1992.

The *World Wide Web* (WWW) uses HTML to send pages of text from one computer to another. The pages may have text, pictures, sound, and video as objects on the page. Certain words, called *hyperlinks,* can take you to another place on the Internet just by clicking on them. It was the ability of the Internet to transmit multimedia pages to your computer that made everyone suddenly get Internet access, and it is probably why you are reading this book right now.

That might be the most technical information you have to read and understand to get started on the Internet. Whatever happens, don't get frustrated while you are exploring. The Internet is a very rapidly changing environment, where what worked yesterday may not work today, and today's technology will be obsolete tomorrow.

Chapter 2

Internet Access

Hardware Requirements

Before you can start surfing the Internet, you must have a computer capable of accessing the Internet. The computer itself is referred to as *hardware,* and the programs that run on the computer are called *software.* Your hardware and software depend on the *operating system* (OS) that you are running.

Two major operating systems are currently in use for home computer users—Windows and Macintosh. You may see these commonly abbreviated as Win and Mac. For simplicity, we will limit ourselves to looking at the Windows system. If you find yourself using a Mac, there are not many significant differences in accessing the Internet from one operating system to another. Windows comes in several versions, Windows 3.1, Windows 95, and Windows NT. Windows 3.1 and 95 are primarily for home computing use, and Windows NT is geared towards networks and businesses. A new version of Windows called Windows 98 is pending release as this book is being written. The numbers after a program name generally refer to the release number; the higher the number, the newer the release. (No, there are not 95 versions of Windows; the "95" represents the year of release and was a marketing strategy.) The operating system is the foundation program that allows all the other programs to run.

A typical computer consists of a *central processing unit* (CPU) and a monitor, or screen. The keyboard allows you to type into the computer, and the mouse is the common tool to navigate around the screen. The *modem* is the connection between your computer and the telephone system.

A few thoughts on computer technology: a faster CPU is not as important as having enough *random access memory* (RAM) to run your programs. RAM is where your computer stores programs that it is currently running. You will probably not notice the speed increase you get from having a faster CPU, but you will notice pretty quickly when your computer crashes because you don't have enough RAM. This is not to be confused with *read only memory* (ROM), which is memory where you cannot store information. This type of memory is reserved for basic operating instructions for the computer, and programs or data cannot be stored there.

Two more important hardware notes: buy the biggest *hard disk* (HD) you can afford. The hard disk is where your computer permanently stores programs or files. The size of programs increases each year, so a HD that seems enormous today may not be large enough tomorrow. Lastly, buy the fastest modem you can afford. At present, modems typically run at speeds of 28,800 or 33,600 *baud,* or bits per second that can be transmitted over the phone line. Modems are now coming out that run at speeds of 56,000 baud. Several new technologies offer alternatives to traditional telephone Internet access, such as cable modems, satellite access, or special telephone lines. Each of these has advantages and disadvantages, and should be thoroughly researched before committing to such a technology.

One final thought on computers: buy the best computer you can afford that does what you need today. The speed of computers generally doubles every 18 months. You will go bankrupt trying to keep up with the current technology, so try to follow the preceding guidelines, and make sure your hardware will perform the tasks you need it to do.

Internet Service Providers

Once you have a computer, you will need an *Internet Service Provider* (ISP). This is a company that you pay to call their computer to access the Internet. There are a few different types of ISPs that you can choose from, and each has advantages and disadvantages.

Any discussion of ISPs must begin with America Online (AOL), the largest commercial ISP in America. About half of all those with Internet access pay for it through AOL. AOL has several payment plans, the most common being $21.95 per month for unlimited access. They also offer plans by the hour or by the year, or where you have Internet access through your work or school. There is a developing trend away from unlimited Internet access for a flat rate, so watch the pricing plans carefully.

Being the largest provider has many advantages. Many people you know may already be on AOL, which makes contacting them very easy. AOL provides a large amount of special content that is not available via the Internet to the general public. AOL is also a worldwide company, which means you can often access them by a local phone call from anywhere. If you travel and need Internet access from the road, or have the potential to relocate permanently, this is a great advantage. You would not need to change your e-mail address if you move; you would simply need to call a new local phone number to access your account.

However, being the largest provider also has some disadvantages. AOL has become infamous recently for busy signals and slow service during peak times, especially since they implemented their unlimited pricing plan. AOL also has had problems with the speed of e-mail delivery between their system and the rest of the Internet. AOL claims to be adding equipment to improve service.

AOL has their Terms of Service, which restricts some activity on their system. They block access to certain sites with objectionable material and make parental control of access very easy. They will revoke your privileges on their system for violations of their Terms of Service, which include posting profanity. To monitor their Terms of Service, AOL may censure you based on postings you make to various forums. E-mail that is sent within the AOL system may also be subject to their Terms of Service.

There are a few other companies like AOL, such as Prodigy and The Microsoft Network (MSN) which offer many of the same features as AOL, but with different content. In the changing world of the Internet, America Online has recently purchased CompuServe, a company that competed for some years with AOL.

If you would rather not use a company such as AOL, you can obtain access to the Internet through another ISP. Companies such as AT&T, MCI, UUNet, and Netcom are large nationwide providers. They do not have the special content that companies such as AOL offer, but they are often faster and more reliable. Most do not block access to any sites, nor do they censure objectionable material (parental controls for minors are widely available). Most ISPs offer an unlimited access pricing plan similar to AOLs.

You can also search out a local ISP where you live. Countless companies provide access near you, though many are actually just middlemen to a large nationwide provider. Internet access from a local provider may be cheaper than from one of the nationwide companies, especially if you purchase a year or more in advance. Any nationwide provider offers the two advantages mentioned earlier: you can often access your account from the road if you travel, and you can keep your account if you relocate. Local providers do not have these advantages, so you will have to weigh the advantages and disadvantages for yourself.

The last major method of obtaining Internet access is through work or school. Many employers and most colleges and universities offer some form of Internet access. This type of access does not usually cost the person anything, but may be available only from work or school. However, there are several disadvantages to Internet access through these means. Your school or employer may restrict your access to certain sites or monitor your online activity. Some accounts are able to view only text, not pictures and other multimedia objects. These accounts are often called *shell accounts*. What's more, when you leave that job or school, you will have to change your e-mail address.

Troubleshooting

Unfortunately, you may find yourself having trouble accessing the Internet. Several common problems can be fixed easily:

- Make sure your modem is set up properly in Windows. External modems should be plugged into the computer and into the electric outlet, and need to be turned on. Internal modems need to be configured properly through software. Make sure that you have properly selected the type of modem you have in Windows.

- Make sure that your Internet program knows the type of modem you have and where it is located. You will need to indicate which communications *(COM)* port, or serial port, the modem is attached to.

- Check the Internet settings for your particular connection. Your ID should be entered properly (lowercase and capital letters matter!). Some programs require you to enter DNS numbers or server names. You should get these directly from your ISP.

- If you have trouble connecting at a high speed, call your telephone company and have them check for noise on the line. Interference caused by static on the telephone line can slow down your connection speeds.

- If you have been connecting to your ISP successfully, but then develop problems, contact your ISP. They may be having temporary technical difficulties, which develop quickly (and are resolved) every day.

Tomorrow's Access

There are two things you should remember about the Internet's always changing nature. One is that as more people get online, you will experience more delays. The bottleneck is usually not on your end; it is the computer you are trying to access. Don't get too frustrated, even when you can't get online when you really need to. Wait a half-hour, and then try again. The bottlenecks tend to go away pretty quickly.

Second, be aware of the new frontiers in Internet access. The technology changes faster than any book can be published, so read a magazine or the newspaper, watch the evening news, or get online to stay up on the newest ways to access the Internet. Things like cable TV modems or digital satellite are being tried out, and tomorrow may bring another revolution in access technology.

Chapter 3

E-Mail

E-Mail Basics

The simplest function of the Internet is electronic mail, or *e-mail*. Most people have had some experience with e-mail, often through their work. Although most work e-mail systems are independent from the Internet, more and more companies are integrating the two.

Internet e-mail addresses have two parts: the name and the domain. The name is the person you are sending the message to, and the domain is the name of the computer where his or her account is located. For example,

bobsmith@netcom.com
reaches "bobsmith" at the computer "netcom.com."

E-mail messages can be sent in one of two formats: text or HTML. Text messages are the most basic, and cannot contain such things as fonts, bold or underlined text, or hyperlinks. However, many simple mail programs cannot read HTML messages. HTML messages offer text formatting and the ability to add hyperlinks to other Internet locations.

Often, files are attached to e-mail messages for transmission across the Internet. For example, you can take a word processing document or a picture that you have, attach it to an e-mail, and send it to someone else. It will take some time, depending on the size of the file you are sending. Then the person you are sending to can download the message and the file attachment. This can be much faster than faxing a large document and allows the recipient to edit the file on his or her computer.

E-Mail Programs

A large number of programs will send and receive e-mail, from the most basic to the very complicated. The program that you will use depends greatly on the ISP from which you are getting your mail. AOL has their own built-in mail system, which works with messages both on the AOL system and to others on the Internet. It is a very simple mail system, with a basic address book. AOL does not currently have mail *filtering*, where messages can be sorted as they are received into folders based on who sent the message or the message subject.

Other ISPs will provide you with a program they choose to access the Internet, such as Microsoft Internet Explorer or Netscape Navigator. Although these programs are primarily used for browsing the World Wide Web (and will be discussed at length later), they both have e-mail functions built in. Other times, you may choose a program you like and configure it yourself, such as Qualcomm Eudora. This process can get fairly complicated though.

Choosing a mail program should be based on what program works best with your ISP. If you are provided with a program, you should stick with it until you become very familiar with Internet operations. Once you are comfortable with the Internet, look around at what program has the best features for the price at the time.

One more option that you can consider. If you need Internet access only in order to send and receive e-mail, there are free services that offer e-mail only. Companies like Juno and Hotmail offer free e-mail, but there are a few conditions. You cannot send or receive file attachments, and you

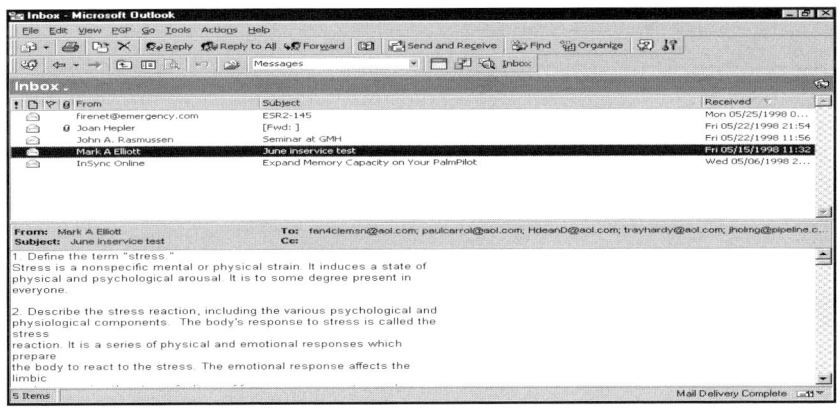

Figure 1   E-Mail on Microsoft Outlook Express.

must tolerate the commercials that are built into the program. And you do not get access to the World Wide Web, Usenet newsgroups, or other Internet features.

E-Mail Etiquette

Although there are many advantages to using e-mail, there are also several disadvantages. The bane of every e-mail account is *spam*. This is unsolicited, bulk e-mail that companies or people send out, usually selling products or services. Often, people get more spam in their mail accounts than actual e-mail. It is very difficult to defeat spam since the technology to create spam improves faster than that designed to beat it.

Here are a few pieces of advice on defeating spam. If you post to a newsgroup, do not include your e-mail address. Some companies have automated programs that search out addresses just to include in the spam lists. Some people recommend not creating a profile on AOL, which tells people something about you personally. If your mail program has a filtering system, you can filter out messages that you know are spam. If you do receive spam, you can try sending a remove message to their server. However, be polite. Some people have found their mailboxes filled with thousands of spam messages when they've complained to the spammer in a threatening manner. Or you can do what most people do: delete the spam and move on.

Another piece of advice: never place anything in an e-mail that you would not want to be read by the general public. With one mouse click, a message can be forwarded to thousands of people, some of whom you might not want to get your message. Some people have inadvertently sent their message to the wrong person or to their entire mailing list. People have found their love letters or hate messages suddenly posted for everyone to see. So always be careful when you type.

You will also see some symbols in messages that you may not have seen before. *Emoticons* are symbols created with punctuation marks that are used to convey a meaning or emotion, like the smiley face :-). Hundreds of combinations of smiley faces are used, each with different meanings. A pretty comprehensive list is available at

http://www.astro.umd.edu/~marshall/smileys.html

Lastly, when you post on the Internet, make sure the Caps Lock button on your computer is off. It's considered impolite, like yelling, to post in all capital letters. If you're lucky, someone will give you a quick lesson in online etiquette. If not, you might find yourself *flamed*, or publicly ridiculed in a very graphic way.

Chapter 4

Newsgroups

Newsgroup Basics

If e-mail is the most basic and widely used part of the Internet, newsgroups are the least used and understood. People who use the Internet every day have never heard of a newsgroup, nevermind used one. But newsgroups, also called Usenet, are a valuable part of the Internet.

A newsgroup is like a bulletin board on a college campus. There are a large number of bulletin boards, more than 18,000 so far. Each bulletin board is for a certain topic, and topics are categorized in similar areas. Any posting on a bulletin board is there for the general public to see, and people can add postings when they want to or just browse what others have posted.

Your ISP subscribes to the newsgroups on a news server, which acts as the campus. The topics and the categories are determined by a central agency. Categories are things like *comp* for computer topics, *gov* for government topics, and *sci* for science topics. You may see public groups like *microsoft* for support for their products, or state or city names that are geographically related. For example, such newsgroups may advertise jobs in a certain area. Countries also have categories, like *uk* for the United Kingdom or *fj* for Japan, and states have categories. The largest category is *alt*, which is where topics that were difficult to classify are listed. The alt group has *binaries*, which are pictures or sounds (some of which are not for younger audiences), fan groups, game discussions, and hundreds of other topics.

In order to find a newsgroup on a certain topic, you can tell your newsreader program to find a certain word or part of a word. Any newsgroups with that word in the title will be indicated for you. Some search engines are also programmed to find news postings, but you will have to select this option. We discuss search engines in Chapter 5.

As with any bulletin board, you can just browse what others have said on the topic or make your own posting. It is recommended that you just browse, or "lurk" in a group for a little while before posting to get the feel of the topic. This also prevents you from asking any questions that have already been asked, which can get you flamed. Newsgroups often have *frequently asked questions* (FAQ) files. Usually, the most common questions asked on a newsgroup have all been compiled for new users. If you do not see the FAQ file on a newsgroup, don't be afraid of asking for it. Some newsgroups are moderated by a supervisor who watches all the postings to make sure they are on the appropriate topic. However, most are just an open forum that takes care of its own content. Off-topic posts do happen and are more common on some newsgroups than on others.

When you make a posting replying to someone else, it is making a *thread*. A thread is a continued discussion on a particular topic within a newsgroup. Usually, threads appear in your news program as indented beneath the original post. This indicates that all these messages are on that particular topic. It is also considered polite to include a quote from the original post when replying to a thread. However, it is considered very impolite to repost a very long message with a one-line comment on the end. This also will likely get you flamed.

Most news servers will let messages expire after a certain time, which depends on how many messages get posted to a particular group. But when you make a posting, it is kept in an archive of messages on the Internet that can be searched by several search engines. People can enter a topic, or your name, and retrieve anything ever posted on that subject, or by you. There is no record of what newsgroups you lurk in, but as soon as you make a posting, it's there forever.

One last word of warning on newsgroups: the content of news postings is generally considered to be open for all, but plagiarism rules still apply. Taking something that you read on a newsgroup and passing it off as your own thought is wrong. But don't believe everything you read on the Internet. Urban legends and falsehoods are quick to circulate on the Internet.

News Reader Programs

In order to read newsgroups on the Internet, you will need to use a newsreader program. As with mail programs, your choice of program will be strongly influenced by your choice of ISP. AOL has their own news program built into their system. Both Internet Explorer and Navigator have

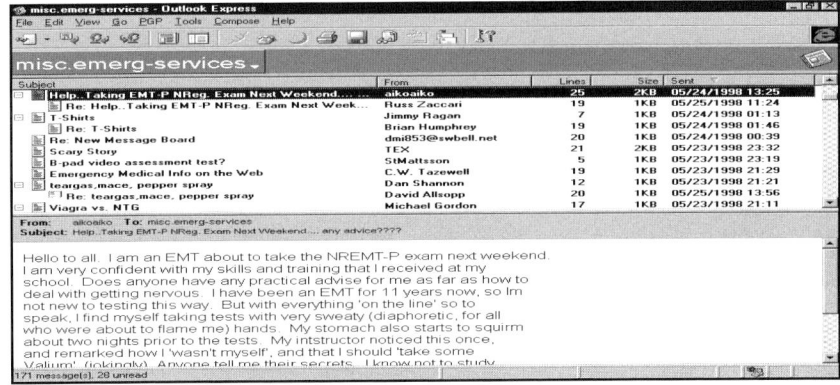

Figure 2 Newsgroups on Microsoft Internet Explorer.

integral news programs also, and many ISPs will give you one of these programs. You may choose another news program if you want, and many are available. But as with mail programs, you will need to configure it yourself, which takes some knowledge and experience.

All news programs will allow you to browse the different newsgroups, read postings, make your own original post or reply to someone else's, or forward a post via e-mail. Some programs are customizable, allowing you to choose certain options. You can view all posts in chronological order or view threaded posts beneath the original message. You can filter out messages from people you don't want to hear from, or from commercial spammers, who can flood newsgroups with unsolicited advertisements.

Most news programs also allow you to download files that may be attached to news messages. Any type of file can be attached to a message—from a binary picture to a word processing document. Usually, you will need to view the downloaded file in a particular program, not the news program itself.

Other News Options

America Online has access to Internet newsgroups, as well as some information centers that only subscribers to AOL can access. These centers are grouped by topic, such as the Public Safety Center. Forums are further categorized into specific areas, such as the EMS/ER Forum and Fire/Rescue Forum. Each forum has a series of topic-sorted newsgroups, which are just like threads, and software libraries of files related to that field. AOL Forums are similar to Internet newsgroups in content and style, but they are all moderated, and you cannot post offensive material (anything that violates AOL's Terms of Service). You can search on AOL for a particular topic and find things that interest you that way.

Another option for getting messages that are all related to a topic is a mailing list, or *Listserv*. As with newsgroups, lists are available for many topics, and some search engines will find you a public mailing list. Lists are usually automated, with a server replying to commands in a certain format. You send a message to subscribe, which will be automatically answered, and then you receive all the messages that are posted. Instead of messages being held on a server where you go to read them, these messages are sent to your mailbox. If you want to make a post, you send a mail message that is forwarded automatically to everyone on the list. Just beware, some lists will generate very high volumes of mail in your inbox.

Chapter 5

World Wide Web

WWW Mechanics

The explosion of content on the Internet is due to the World Wide Web (WWW). This feature is based on the concept of hypertext. Hypertext uses HTML to create a page that can have text, pictures, sound, and video as objects to be viewed. Some of the words or objects may be hyperlinks, which can transport you to another page on the WWW by clicking on them.

Think of the Internet as one huge computer. On your computer, if you want to find a document, you would open up your word processor, then tell the computer to open a document you are looking for located on your hard disk. Similarly, the Internet allows you to open documents located in specific places on other computers, and those documents can be hypertext.

One of the most frustrating things about the WWW is how it changes daily. A document that you want to look for may have been moved or deleted. The WWW is also not very forgiving of errors. If you want to open a document on your computer, you have to tell it very specifically where to look, for example, c:\documents\brady\chapter5.doc. On the WWW, you tell your web browser to look for **http://www.prenhall.com/bradybooks/search.html**. This tells the computer to use the *hypertext transfer protocol* (HTTP) to go to the computer at www.prenhall.com, go to the directory bradybooks, and open the document called search.html. This is why things have to be entered exactly. The Internet address is called a *uniform resource locator* (URL).

WWW Programs

One of the most critical aspects of accessing the Internet is the program you use. As a word processor opens up documents for you to read and change, a web *browser* opens web pages for you to read. In fact, most new browsers open up all sorts of files. This is a requirement since the average web page may have text in HTML, a picture in .JPEG format, sounds in .WAV format, and a banner that was written in *Java*.

The first web browser that was designed to read pages in HTML was called Mosaic. Today, two major browsers hold a vast majority of the market: Internet Explorer from Microsoft and Navigator from Netscape. Each of them has comparable functions, so preference may be personal. Until recently, the largest difference was price, since Internet Explorer was free, but you needed to purchase Navigator unless you were a student. However, Netscape just made Navigator a free product also—continuing the ever-changing environment that is the Internet. Both of these programs offer built-in modules for e-mail and newsgroups, as well as other options.

Each browser lets you select a home page. This page is the first thing you will see when you open up your browser. It can be a page set by the program, a page selected by your ISP, or another page you select. The home page may allow you to link to other pages, read the daily news, or perform Internet searches.

Each browser also allows you to remember your favorite places, so you will not have to type in the URL every time you want to visit a page. The programs will remember a list of favorite places, or bookmarks. The programs also allow you to select certain options, such as the level of security, colors, or number of recently visited sites to remember.

Figure 3 Microsoft Internet Explorer 4.0 Web Browser.

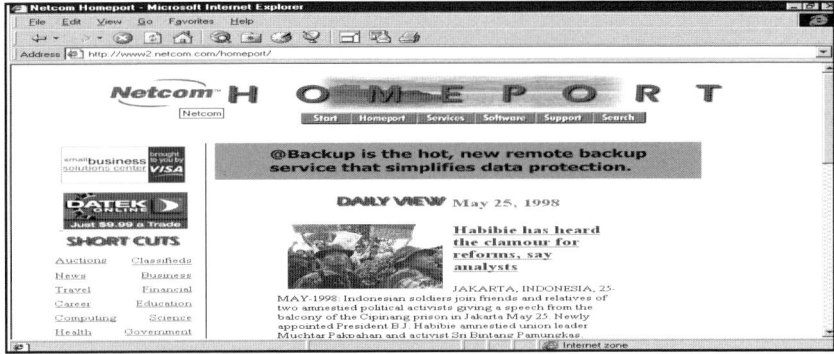

Figure 4 A Home Page.

In order to use a browser program, you will need to learn how to use its toolbar. Across the top of the program window, just above where you view the web page, will be a series of buttons. There are buttons for back and forward, which will take you to the last web page you visited in that direction. There is a stop button, which stops any activity your browser is performing. This is useful when a page is taking a very long time to download or when you want to interrupt an action. The reload button tells the browser to refresh the current page you are viewing, and the home button takes you back to your selected home page. Each browser program has several other buttons that perform specific functions, such as selecting a search engine, opening up your favorite sites, or printing out a web page.

All browser programs also have an address window, where the exact URL of the web page you are viewing is displayed. When you hyperlink to a web site, the URL in the address window changes auto-

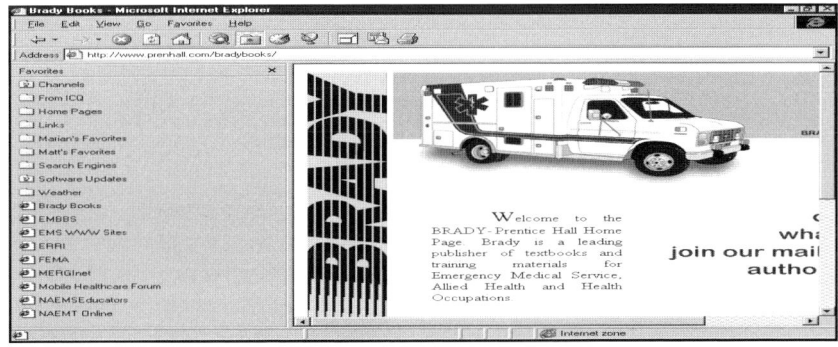

Figure 5 Favorite Places in Internet Explorer.

matically. However, if you know the exact address of a web site you want to visit, you can just type it directly into the address window. But be careful—you need to get the address exactly right!

Browsers also allow you to download programs from the Internet. You may link automatically to some downloads, or you may find yourself in a file transfer protocol (FTP) site. An FTP site may look like a traditional directory on a computer, and from it, you can select the subdirectory you want to look in. Just click on the branch of the tree you want to go to until you reach your destination.

Search Engines

There is a lot of information on the WWW. Some of it comes and goes, and some computers are not always working properly. But even considering those factors, it can take time to find what you're looking for. When you're looking for something, you may end up finding everything but what you started out toward.

Search engines are designed to make this process easier. There are a large number of search engines, such as Yahoo!, Excite, Infoseek, and Lycos. Search engines are web pages that have lists of other web pages indexed by keywords. You can go to the search page and put in the things you are looking for, and the search engine will report to you anything it finds with those keywords. Each search engine compiles a different list of web sites and searches it differently, so you might want to try a few search engines if you don't find what you're looking for the first time.

Unfortunately, you may find the curse of the Internet when you try to find something. Either you can't find anything at all on a subject, or you find so much stuff it's overwhelming. If you don't get any "hits" on a topic, try different search engines or different keywords.

Figure 6 Lycos Search Engine.

Sometimes looking at a subject from a slightly different angle will solve this problem.

The problem of finding too much information is much harder to fix. The first thing to try is using more than one keyword, which may narrow down the results. You will also need to be careful about what you use as a keyword because you will get returns on anything *at all* with that word included. If you run an Infoseek search for the word *Brady* because you are looking for the Brady Books Home Page, you will find that five of the first ten hits are related to the TV show "The Brady Bunch." One of the pages is for a family named Brady, one is about the Brady Bill, one is for the Brady USA company, and one is seemingly unrelated. Instead, if you search on *Brady Books,* you will find the third page on the list is the Brady Books Prentice Hall Home Page.

The way in which you type your request into a search engine is very important. If you type in three words for the search engine to find, it will find web pages with any of those three words. Of course, the results should be ranked, with the pages with all words listed above those with only one or two. If you want to find pages that have all three words only, put the phrase in quotation marks. The search engine will now find pages with that exact phrase. There are other tricks to narrowing down your search. The commands AND, OR, and NOT can indicate more accurately which words you want to include or exclude from the search. Becoming proficient at searching is a learned skill that you will get better at over time.

Another trick to finding things you are looking for is to find one page that has related information. Most web pages have an area called *links,* where they list hyperlinks to other sites that are related to the one where you currently are located. Any "Brady Bunch" web page will probably have a listing of links to other "Brady Bunch" web pages.

There are also some search pages dedicated to finding e-mail and telephone listings, such as four11.com and whowhere.com. These pages have specific search pages for e-mail addresses, residential phone listings, and commercial phone listings. The pages are so sophisticated now that you can actually access a map showing you where an address you found is located.

Interesting Sites

So where do you start? Considering that this book was published by Brady Publishing, you might want to take a look at the Brady Books Home Page located at **http://www.bradybooks.com**. Here you can find an online catalog of all the publications offered by Brady Publishing, a copy of the Author's Guidelines in case you want to write your own book, a list of what's new at Brady, and e-mail addresses to contact individuals at Brady. It's a well-designed, simple, and easy-to-use page.

To get an idea of the unbelievable volume of information on the Internet, try going to **http://cnn.com**. The Cable News Network has up-to-date information on an endless series of topics, complete with downloadable movie clips. If you want to find out the weather in an area of the country, click on their weather page. You can get a five-day forecast, as well as animated weather radar for that area of the world.

One of the most powerful services the Internet offers is helping you conduct a job search. Some jobs are advertised only on the Internet. One of the biggest sites is FedWorld, the federal government's job announcement site. Located at **http://www.fedworld.com**, you will find a searchable listing of jobs throughout the country. Just put in a keyword, like *paramedic,* and you get a listing of all jobs available for paramedics in the federal system. You will find the location, description, and salary offered for any posted positions. This is one example of the many sites dedicated to matching you up with your dream job.

Considering that you are using a computer, you may find the need for additional software. Most software companies make *patches* and updates to their programs available on their web sites. Other sites, such as **http://www.windows95.com**, have shareware and freeware programs. Shareware programs are written and made available for you to try, either with some features disabled or with an expiration date. Freeware programs are written and made available for free, just as the name says. Windows95.com has many programs available for you to try that are utilities, games, tools, and Internet programs.

The number of WWW pages available cannot be estimated accurately. Every day pages are posted, and others are removed. The information is constantly being updated. On many pages, there will be a message that says when the page was last updated, which will indicate how accurate the information is. The topics available are also enormous in number. Your favorite airline and special interest group can be found online. You can buy almost anything on the WWW—from greeting cards to flowers to music to software. Most government agencies have home pages, where you can get information directly online or have publications sent to you.

Internet Security

There are a few things you should know about your security and privacy when surfing the web. One of the most important things that you can do to protect yourself when connected to the Internet is to purchase a good commercial antivirus program. Many different brands are on the market, and just about all of them will protect you against downloading a virus that will wipe out all of your data. The better virus protection programs have a module that runs continuously in the background looking for suspicious activity. This is important because a virus can quickly wipe you out, often before you have had time to run your antivirus program. Another important feature is to be able to download free virus updates from the program's manufacturer. New viruses are invented every day, and you should update your virus signatures at least monthly.

There are other ways in which you should protect yourself on the Internet. When you visit a web site, a file called a *cookie* can be placed on your hard disk. This cookie contains information about your Internet connection, what sites you have visited, and what you are looking for on that particular web site. Cookies can be very useful by saving preferences about how you like to view a web site or saving passwords so that you don't have to enter them each time you visit a page. But information is present in each cookie that you may not always want to make available. Most new browsers allow you to reject or accept cookies, either overall or individually. Consider activating this function so that you can monitor which sites are sending you cookies, and how often.

Remember when browsing the web that a great deal of information about you is available online. If you go to a search engine, you can probably find your address, phone number, and e-mail address very easily. Each time you offer information on the Internet, it will be stored somewhere. It may come back as junk mail or spam. This is not to say that you should not browse the web or offer information about yourself. Just be careful of what information you offer and where you offer it.

One last word of warning: a great deal of press has been dedicated to Internet security and online commerce. There is some danger in purchasing something on the Internet with a credit card. A criminal could intercept your credit card number and charge something illegally. Some safeguards are in place to prevent this from happening. Most browsers have a secure mode, where data is encrypted to prevent it from being intercepted. Most credit card companies will track down any fraud that is brought to their attention with a minimum of liability to you, the cardholder. Consider the risk involved in making online purchases compared to giving your credit card to a waiter in a restaurant, who could easily copy down the number for future use. Although there is a risk involved with online commerce, it is certainly very low.

Chapter 6

EMS Internet Resources

WWW Pages

So, now you know all about the Internet. You just need to know where to start. A great deal of EMS-related information is available on the Internet. Many agencies have established home pages, which give information about their history, how they operate, and their personnel. The most comprehensive listing of all the EMS web pages on the Internet can be found at **http://www.district.north-van.bc.ca/eswsl/Www-911.htm**. This is the Emergency Services WWW List, which has categorized links to every EMS-related page that they find out about.

But you are looking for real, usable information. You want to stay on the cutting edge of EMS, with the most current material available. Unfortunately, there are fewer sites with solid information than you would think. One of the newest sites is the Mobile Healthcare Forum (MHF) at **http://www.mhf.net**. This site has several unique features. It has a conference center, where discussions are conducted on certain EMS topics. The conference center also has chat sessions (often with well-known EMS lecturers and researchers), polls, and surveys. There is a mall with stores from EMS product and service companies. An online university offers distance education, including the National EMS Quality and Performance Workshop and the National EMS Medical Directors Course. The university is also establishing an EMS benchmarking network. A library has links to online books and journals, government documents, and search engines. You can find an online listing of all the links in this book on the Mobile Healthcare Forum site at **http://www.mhf.net/library/booksupport/Bradyinternet.htm**.

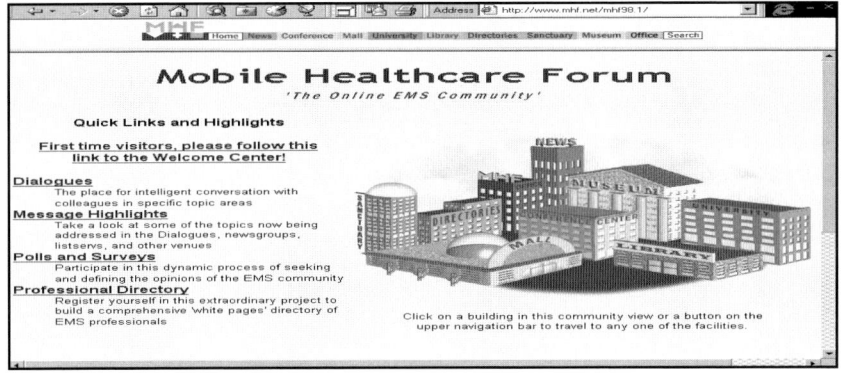

Figure 7   Mobile Healthcare Forum.

There are other sections to the Mobile Healthcare Forum, such as a directory of EMS personnel (where you can register yourself), an EMS museum, a stress-debriefing center, and a news center. This site has some of the most innovative content on the Internet—easy to use and navigate and very up to date. This site became active only in March 1998, so some of the sections are still being constructed. The more people who visit this site, the more important and invaluable it will become.

Another one of the most innovative sites is the Emergency Response and Research Institute (ERRI) at **http://www.emergency.com**. ERRI has the most accurate and comprehensive emergency services news available. Some of the ERRI services are for a fee, such as a daily e-mail directly to your mailbox with the day's domestic and international news. Most of the information can be accessed directly from the web site and is categorized into fire, police, and EMS operations pages, graphics, disaster and rescue, hazardous materials, and other specialties. ERRI also stays current on the political arena and terrorist incidents that are part of the emergency response environment.

One of the most valuable features you can find at ERRI is their Lessons On Line. Presently, two lessons are available: Chemical/Biological Attack and Integrated Emergency Management. These are scenarios, put together by people who have been in the business, with links to other related Internet resources as well as a final quiz. The scenarios are realistic and will make you think about issues you may not have considered before.

The federal government's lead agency for emergency services and consequence management is FEMA, the Federal Emergency Management Agency. Their web page, at **http://www.fema.gov**, has some

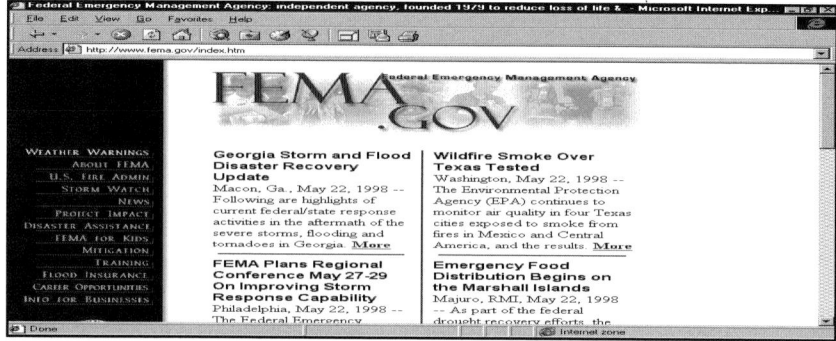

Figure 8   Federal Emergency Management Agency.

valuable information available. Their Learning Resource Center has an online card catalog, so you can search for information on a subject related to emergency services. Downloadable documents from FEMA are available in Adobe PDF (portable document format). The Adobe Acrobat Reader for PDF documents is also available online for no charge.

The Medical, Emergency, Rescue, and Global Information Network (MERGInet) is at **http://www.merginet.com**. This site has several important features, such as a daily headline search for healthcare issues. There are articles written just for MERGInet on various emergency services topics, discussions, classifieds, and a very important resource. A free MedLine search is available from MERGInet, which runs a search of a large number of medical journals for peer-reviewed research articles.

One of the best web sites available for medical information is the Emergency   Medicine   and   Primary   Care   Homepage   at **http://www.embbs.com**. If you have any interest in clinical emergency medicine, this is the place for you. It's like medical school online. You can

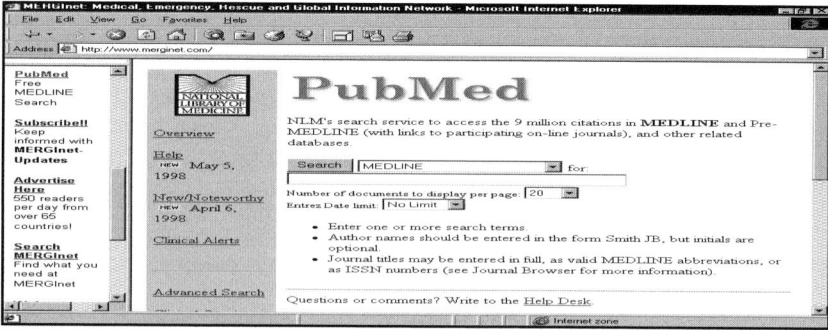

Figure 9   MedLine Search.

find case studies, radiology and medical photograph libraries, and other clinical information. Of course, there are the ever-present job listings and links to other sites. One of the unique features of this site is its ACLS and PALS Megacode Simulators, where you are walked through an interactive patient–care scenario in real time. Take your time when you visit this site: there is a lot to see and a lot to learn.

An outstanding medical search engine called HealthAtoZ is located at **http://www.healthatoz.com**. It has structured links to many health-care-related sites, including some related to EMS. There are also some message boards and news sections to this site.

Two EMS organizations have outstanding web pages. The National Association of EMTs (NAEMT) web page is at **http://www.naemt.org**. You will find many features here, including membership and award information. Two important features of this web site are information on the Public Safety Officers Benefit Program and information on the National Moment of Silence Project. NAEMT is very active in taking care of the families of those providers who have lost their lives while taking care of others. The National Association of EMS Educators (NAEMSE) page is at **http://www.naemse.org**. This site includes information for education specialists, although you will need to be a member of NAEMSE to access some forums.

The two largest publications in EMS are *JEMS Magazine* and *Emergency Medical Services Magazine*. The *JEMS Magazine* home page is at **http://www.jems.com**, and has one of the best classified advertisements sections available, especially for job listings. At present, they do not offer a searchable database of past articles, nor do they offer text of articles online. *Emergency Medical Services Magazine* is at **http://www.ems-magazine.com**, and has made some texts of articles available. Both sites have other information online, such as subscription sign-up and conference information.

Newsgroups

A number of Usenet newsgroups are available on the Internet. Your Internet provider may not subscribe to every one but should subscribe to at least a few of these:

- News:misc.emerg-services—EMS and Fire Discussions
- News:alt.med.ems—Primarily EMS Discussions
- News:alt.firefighters—Firefighting Discussions
- News:alt.emergency.services.dispatcher—EMS and Fire Communications

- News:bit.listserv.fire-l—Firefighting Discussions
- News:gov.us.topic.emergency.misc—FEMA Notices of Disaster Declarations

Mailing Lists

Many more mailing lists are available than are listed here. Each Listserv has a set of commands for how to subscribe or make postings. Usually, you send a command to the address listed here, and in the body of the text, type "subscribe [your e-mail address]." For some of the lists, you will need to specify which of the lists on that server you want to subscribe to, and then include your e-mail address.

- EMED-L@ITSSRV1.UCSF.EDU—Emergency Medicine Mailing List
- EMERG-L@VM.MARIST.EDU—Emergency Services Discussion
- EMERGENCY-MANAGEMENT@LISTSERV.AOL.COM— Emergency Management Coordinators
- LEPC@LIST.UVM.EDU—Hazardous Materials Emergency Response Planning
- PUBLICSAFETYNEWS@LISTSERV.AOL.COM—Public Safety and Emergency Services
- EMS-L@listserv.ACNS.NWU.EDU—Emergency Medicine from National Association of EMS Physicians
- listserv@mediccom.org—Several Lists:
  SITREPS—Situation Reports for Disasters
  DMATNEWS—Disaster Medical Assistance Team Development
  HAZMED—Hazardous Materials Medicine
  DISMED—Disaster Medicine
  TERRORISM—Emergency Response to Terrorism
- USAR@HOME.EASE.LSOFT.COM—Urban Search and Rescue Task Forces

You can search the Internet on most search engines by specifying your topic and Listserv as the search strings. You will find that a very large number of mailing lists are available. Some of them will flood your inbox with mail, whereas others send out only a few messages each day. Some of them have great information and discussions, whereas others lack helpful information.

Other Internet Features

Real-Time Interaction

One of the best features of the Internet is the ability to keep in touch with friends and colleagues, and to do it cheaply. It costs a lot of money to talk on the phone, so here are a few other options.

America Online has "Buddy Lists." You can add the screen names of everyone you want to keep in touch with to a window, and whenever you are online at the same time as your friends, their screen names will appear in the window. This way, you can carry on a conversation in real time. But you don't talk, you type. A screen opens up where you type messages back and forth. So, for the price of a local phone call to AOL, you can talk to someone and have him or her answer you immediately.

For people who do not have AOL, there are two alternatives. The first is called ICQ by Mirablis, which is a take-off on I Seek You. This program is similar to Buddy Lists and works as long as the person you want to chat with also has ICQ installed. The program runs in the background while you are on the Internet, and tells you as soon as someone you are looking for is online at the same time as you. Then you can carry on a written dialogue. ICQ can be downloaded from **http://www.mirablis.com**.

AOL decided that they would get into the market for those people who do not have AOL. They invented the Instant Messenger, which is just like a Buddy List or ICQ. The Instant Messenger allows AOL members to chat with those on the Internet, or two people on the Internet can chat without ever having to be on AOL. Internet Messenger can be downloaded from **http://www.aol.com**.

These two programs are free for you to download and install. You need only make sure that your friends are all using the same program

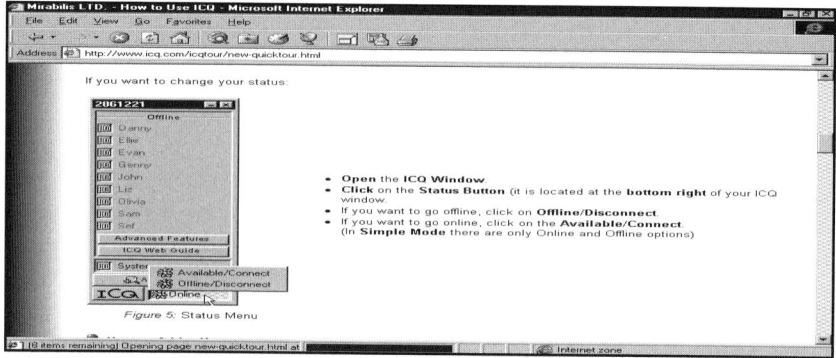

Figure 10 ICQ by Mirablis.

and have your ID number or name. However, one word of warning: people will often look for others to prey on via real-time interactions. A number of people have been duped by requests for their password or billing information. Other times, people are harassed by others when they want to be left alone. All these programs have features that allow you to warn others or block them from seeing you or sending you messages.

These programs are all variations on the theme of chat. There are many ways to chat, both on AOL and on the Internet itself. Chatting on the Internet itself is often called Internet relay chat (IRC). There are chat rooms where many people get together and type messages back and forth. Many of these rooms are organized by topic, and some are not for younger viewers. One more warning: people are not necessarily who they portray themselves to be in a chat. The person who identifies himself as Tom Cruise or herself as Cindy Crawford probably is not.

For those of you who need to actually talk, not just send text back and forth, there are other options. You may have heard about Internet phone, where you carry on a voice conversation through your computer on the Internet. This way, you pay only local charges for a long-distance or international call. You can download free programs that allow you to do this, such as NetMeeting from Microsoft. However, you will need a computer that is configured to allow two-way conversations in full duplex. Otherwise, you will be able only to talk or listen, but not both at the same time. You will also need a fast Internet connection. The quality involved at a 28,800 or 33,600 baud connection is not great, so you will need at least a 56,000 baud connection to have a good conversation. And both of you will need the fast connection and the Internet phone program.

Chapter 8

The Future of the Internet

The Internet is a rapidly changing place. Every day web pages are added and deleted, and newsgroups and Listservs are invented. The technology of the Internet is always improving, offering better methods of connecting your computer to an ISP and faster speeds. Programs such as web browsers and e-mail clients are released or improved frequently. And soon the information in this book will be out of date.

Don't become discouraged. You will have bad Internet days, where you can't get your computer to connect, or you can't find that piece of information you need most. Perhaps you are not searching in the right place, or what you want is not yet available online. Remember the nature of the Internet, and keep at it.

One of the most rapidly changing areas of the Internet is the ISPs. Much of the discussion about ISPs concerns America Online versus a traditional ISP. Personally, I have used both types extensively and prefer a traditional nationwide ISP. This is not to say that AOL may not be your best choice, especially if you are an Internet beginner. Always remember that you can change your ISP without much trouble, especially as prices or customer service change.

Finally, keep your eyes open for newspaper articles or other information about the Internet. Considering how quickly things change on the Internet, you will want to make sure that you are up to date on any major changes that occur. Big things are happening, with online commerce expanding each day and Congress considering legislation that could drastically affect your Internet service. So watch for current events, and good luck on your Internet adventures.

Glossary

Baud   Bits per second—a measure of how fast information is transmitted from one computer to another over telephone lines.

Binary   A picture or sound file that is transmitted between computers on the Internet.

Browser   The program used to view HTML pages on the web.

Client–Server Network   Connection of computers where a client computer requests a file or piece of information from a central computer, or server.

COM Port   Communications port—also known as a serial port, where a communications device is connected to your computer.

Cookie   A file placed on your computer by a web page that contains information about your Internet connection, your browsing preferences, or what web sites you have visited.

CPU   Central processing unit—the computer chip that controls the computer's operation.

DNS   Domain name system—the four groups of numbers, separated by periods, that are domain names when translated for use by Internet computers.

Domain   The individual name of each computer connected to the Internet.

DOS   Disk operating system—the text-based operating system that was the original foundation of Windows.

E-Mail   Electronic mail—allows short messages to be sent from one person to another via computers.

Emoticons Symbols created with punctuation marks that have meanings, like the smiley face :-).

FAQ Frequently asked questions—the most common questions asked on a newsgroup that have been compiled for new users.

Filtering Sorting of e-mail messages into specific folders based on who sent it or the subject line.

Flamed Publicly ridiculed on an electronic forum for something you have posted.

FTP File transfer protocol—a method of transferring files from one computer to another through the Internet.

Hardware The computer and its components.

HD Hard disk—the magnetic disk where the computer permanently stores programs or information.

HTML Hypertext markup language—the language used to write web pages, which can contain links to other pages, graphics, sound, and video.

HTTP Hypertext transfer protocol—the computer language that is used to transfer hypertext (HTML) from one computer to another.

Hyperlink HTML text lines that take you to another place on the Internet by clicking on them.

Hypertext See *HTML.*

Internet A connection of computers from schools, companies, governments, and other agencies that use the same language to communicate.

IRC Internet relay chat—a method for two or more people to communicate by text directly to each other in real time.

ISP Internet service provider—a company whose computer is connected directly to the Internet. These companies will allow you to connect to the Internet through their computer for a fee.

Java A language used on web pages to perform simple functions, such as create a banner that scrolls a message across the page.

Listserv Messages on a specific topic that are sent directly to your e-mail account, instead of having to read them on a newsgroup.

Mac Macintosh—a computer and operating system, where actions can be taken by selecting objects with a mouse.

Modem The device that allows the connection between a computer and the telephone system.

Newsgroups Public forums for posting messages for others to read and reply to on a specific subject. Also known as Usenet.

Operating System   The foundation program that allows all the other programs to run.

Packet Data Transfer   Method of transmitting information between computers where a message is broken down into smaller pieces, which are sent through many servers en route to the destination computer.

Patches   Updates or repairs to programs that are available on the Internet, usually written by the program's manufacturer.

RAM   Random access memory—memory where the computer stores programs or information that is currently in use.

ROM   Read only memory—memory that cannot be written to and where basic instructions for the computer are stored.

Software   The programs that run on the computer.

Spam   Unsolicited bulk e-mail messages, usually selling products or services.

TCP/IP   Transmission control protocol/Internet protocol—the universal language used by all computers on the Internet to communicate.

Thread   A continued discussion on a particular topic within a news-group.

UNIX   A text-based language in which most early Internet work was done.

URL   Uniform resource locator—the Internet address where a web page can be found.

Usenet   See *Newsgroups.*

Windows   An operating system used by most home computers, where actions can be taken by selecting objects with a mouse.

WWW   World Wide Web—the sharing of HTML documents between computers.